This is the second of the Henry Mouse books
The first: Henry Mouse: A Christmas Tale
and the third: Henry Mouse and the Zoo Adventure are
also now available on Amazon Books.

# Henry Mouse is trying again

**A tale of invention and imagination
Written by Andy Harden
and illustrated by Paul Davies**

Andy Harden is a writer, and teaching assistant in
Gloucester where he works in a primary school
(he thinks it keeps him young).
This book is dedicated to his wife Sally,
the memory of his son Marcus
and all the children he works with.

Paul Davies is a cartoonist, illustrator, cook and allotment gardener.
His part of the book is dedicated to his grandchildren:
Wilfred, Sidney, Elliot and Finley.

Outside the day was bright and warm
The sun was shining down
And Henry mouse was in his house
A hole just underground

Now Henry thought that he might try
To see if mice were meant to fly
Without the aid of petrol motor
Or a helicopter rotor

In his house he hid away
He worked and worked on Saturday
Until there was a grand revealing
When his friends did hurt his feelings
They said "it will never fly"
Though it was "a right good try"

But Henry knew that he was right
And that soon he would take flight
So he put on his flying gear
Showing not a trace of fear

There it stood his grand contraption
Full of pulley interaction
Flappy wings he'd made of wood
Which he said were "very good"
Bits of string and knotted cable
And a leg from Henry's table

It was big from port to starboard
With a cockpit made of cardboard
"Right" he said "it's time to try it
I need height so I can fly it"

With helpful friends his wish fulfilled
They pulled it up a local hill
And at the top he clambered in
Tightened ropes and checked the string

While they watched in admiration
At this mouse and his creation
With a leg out of each side
Off he went with two big strides

Flapping with his wings to try
To find the wind to help him fly
But though he flapped and flapped again
His flapping seemed to be in vain

But then he jumped and left the ground
And making funny squeaking sounds
He soared away and out of view
Off he went he really flew

Away from them he dipped and soared
While down below they whooped and roared
Until he disappeared from view
Into a cloud brave Henry flew

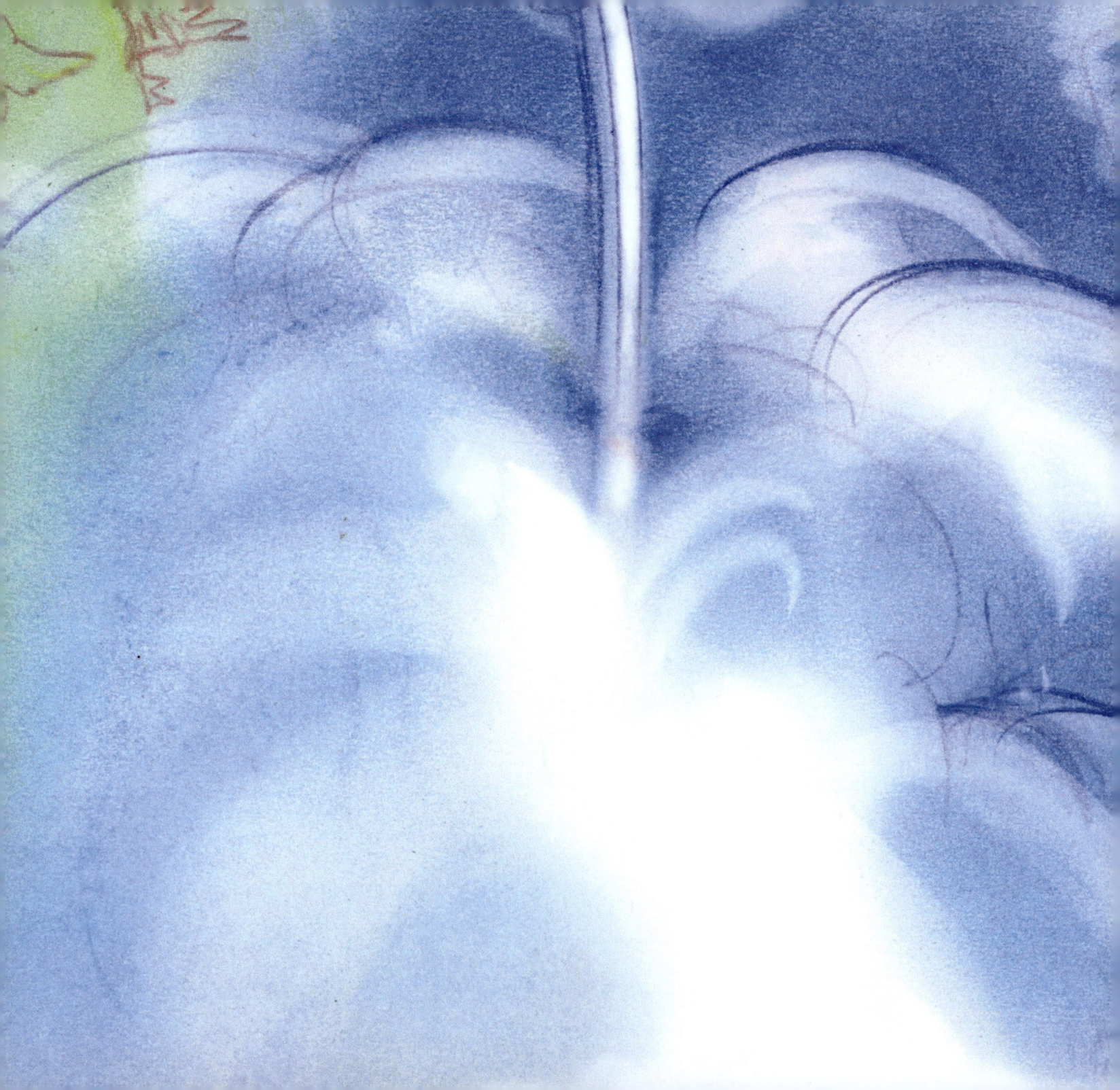

His friends both looked and stared in vain
They could not see that little plane
He was gone flown out of sight
So had he really conquered flight?

No! As then they heard him calling
And they both could see him falling
"It doesn't work" he sadly shouted
"I was wrong, no doubt about it"

But he did not suffer harm
As he landed near a farm
He came to Earth at ten to two
Saved by a pile of old cow poo!

His special friends both helped him home
He had a bath with extra foam
And while he washed his furry face
He thought "I tried there's no disgrace"
So with that thought inside his head
Henry took himself to bed.

The moral of this tale is true
When you're trying something new
If at first you don't succeed
Don't get upset there is no need
For you can have another go
And next time well,
you never know...

Printed in Dunstable, United Kingdom